Confront Conflicts

The Path to a Successful Marriage

I0459693

Hope Grace

PUBLISHING

Alexandria, Virginia, USA

By **Hope Grace**

Published by Hope Grace Publishing
HopeGracePublishing.com
Alexandria, Virginia, USA

This book is a work of nonfiction. While the author has made every effort to ensure accuracy and clarity, some names, details, and events have been changed to protect the privacy of individuals. Any resemblance to actual persons, living or dead, is purely coincidental.

ISBN: 978-1-966423-23-2
Library of Congress Control Number: 2024926897

First Edition: 2025

Dedication

To Paul,

For walking this journey with me — for your love, patience, and willingness to grow alongside me. Every challenge we faced has brought us closer, and I am forever grateful for the strength we found in each other.

To all couples who choose to face conflict with courage and love — may this book serve as a reminder that every disagreement holds the potential for deeper understanding and connection.

Contents

Introduction

When I first got married, I thought I knew what a healthy relationship looked like. I had read books, listened to advice, and watched couples who seemed to have it all figured out. But no amount of preparation could have equipped me for the reality of navigating conflicts in a marriage. It didn't take long for me to realize that a successful partnership isn't defined by the absence of conflict — it's about how those conflicts are handled.

The inspiration for this book comes from personal experiences and countless conversations with friends. In my own marriage, I faced challenges that, at times, seemed insurmountable. Yet, these challenges became opportunities to grow, both as individuals and as a couple. Talking with friends, I realized that many couples face similar struggles — misunderstandings, emotional disconnects, and a fear of confronting issues head-on. These shared experiences showed me the universal nature of these challenges and the importance of addressing them with honesty and intention.

One of the most pervasive myths I encountered — both in my marriage and in these conversations — was the idea that avoiding conflict or "letting the other win" was the key to marital harmony. This approach may create temporary peace, but it often leads to long-term dissatisfaction. Avoiding conflict doesn't make the problems go away; it simply buries them, allowing resentment to fester beneath the surface.

Take, for example, a recurring disagreement between my husband Paul and me. Early in our marriage, he believed that "letting me win" whenever I got angry would de-escalate our arguments. But his retreat felt dismissive, as if my feelings didn't matter enough to engage with. For years, I tried to make him understand that my anger wasn't a loss of control but a signal that something important needed to be addressed. Ignoring those signals only widened the gap between us.

At the beginning of our marriage, I often told Paul, "As long as I'm still fighting, you should be happy because it means I have not given up on our marriage. If someday you find me stop fighting yet unhappy, you should worry because that means I don't care anymore and am ready to quit the marriage." He eventually took my words to heart and gradually wasn't so eager to avoid conflicts. This shift marked the beginning of real growth in our relationship.

Over time, Paul and I learned a vital truth: avoiding conflict is not the same as resolving it. True marital success comes from addressing the underlying issues that spark disagreements. It's about facing uncomfortable conversations, validating each other's feelings, and working together to find solutions. With each confrontation we faced, we grew stronger as a couple, building trust and understanding along the way.

In this book, I will share stories from my marriage — some humorous, some frustrating, and all deeply personal. These stories illustrate how addressing conflicts, rather than avoiding them, can transform a relationship. Whether it's a disagreement over something as small as folding socks or as emotionally charged as feeling dismissed in a conversation, every conflict carries an opportunity for growth.

By exploring these experiences, I hope to show that conflicts are not threats to a marriage but opportunities to build a deeper, more resilient connection. Together, we will challenge the myths about conflict, learn strategies for addressing underlying issues, and discover the transformative power of confrontation. If you're ready to embrace conflict as a path to greater understanding and love, then this book is for you.

Part 1: Understanding Conflict in Marriage

Chapter 1: What Conflict Really Is

Conflict in marriage is inevitable. Two people with different personalities, backgrounds, and perspectives will naturally have disagreements. Yet, many of us enter marriage with the hope that if we find the right person, conflict will be minimal or nonexistent. This expectation, though comforting, is far from reality.

The truth is, conflict itself is not the problem. It's how we approach and handle it that determines whether it becomes a destructive force or a tool for growth. Understanding the nature of conflict is the first step to navigating it effectively.

The Difference Between Healthy and Unhealthy Conflict

Healthy conflict is about addressing issues, expressing emotions, and working toward solutions. It's driven by a mutual desire to understand and support one another. While it may involve uncomfortable conversations or heated emotions, the goal is to resolve misunderstandings and strengthen the relationship.

Unhealthy conflict, on the other hand, is characterized by blame, avoidance, or escalation. Instead of seeking resolution, it creates emotional distance, resentment, and hurt. Examples include constant criticism, refusing to engage in dialogue, or using conflict as a means to dominate or control. Recognizing this distinction is crucial for fostering constructive interactions.

Why Conflict Is a Natural Part of Marriage

Conflict is a natural byproduct of closeness. When two individuals share a life, their differing needs, expectations, and habits inevitably clash. Far from being a sign of incompatibility, conflict is evidence of the dynamic and evolving nature of relationships.

For example, when Paul and I got married, we quickly realized how differently we approached seemingly small matters, such as folding socks or handling the sound system. These everyday conflicts were not signs of a failing relationship — they were opportunities to learn about each other's preferences and communicate better. Instead of avoiding these moments, we began to view them as chances to grow closer by understanding one another more deeply.

Misconceptions About Conflict and Anger

One of the biggest misconceptions about conflict is that it should be avoided at all costs. Many people equate conflict with failure or believe that a happy marriage is one free of disagreements. This myth can lead couples to suppress their feelings, creating an illusion of peace while underlying issues remain unresolved. Over time, this avoidance fosters resentment and emotional disconnection.

Anger is another misunderstood aspect of conflict. Many view anger as inherently negative — a loss of control that should be hidden or avoided. But anger is often a signal that something important needs attention. For me, expressing anger wasn't a sign of being irrational or out of control; it was my way of asking Paul to address an issue that mattered to me.

Viewing my anger as a loss of control is an underestimation of me. Once Paul changed his perspective of anger from a destructive force to a constructive one, it became easier for us to engage in productive discussions.

This shift in perspective wasn't immediate. It took time and persistence for Paul to recognize that my anger was rooted in care for our relationship, not hostility. When he began to approach our disagreements with curiosity rather than avoidance, our discussions transformed. We were no longer trying to "win" arguments but instead worked to understand each other better.

By embracing conflict as a natural and even necessary part of marriage, couples can shift their perspective from fearing disagreements to seeing them as opportunities for growth. In the next chapters, we will explore how to recognize and validate emotions, address underlying issues, and transform conflict into a tool for building a stronger, more resilient relationship.

Chapter 2: The Role of Cultural and Personal Backgrounds

Every individual enters marriage carrying a unique set of experiences, values, and habits shaped by their upbringing. These personal and cultural backgrounds play a significant role in shaping how we approach conflict. Understanding these influences is key to navigating disagreements and fostering mutual respect in a marriage.

How Upbringing Shapes Conflict Resolution Styles

The way we respond to conflict often stems from what we observed and experienced growing up. Some people come from families where conflicts were openly discussed, creating an environment where healthy communication was modeled. Others may have grown up in households where disagreements were avoided or dealt with through shouting and emotional outbursts. These early experiences heavily influence how we approach disagreements as adults.

For example, in Paul's family, open communication was not encouraged. Conflicts were often swept under the rug to maintain the appearance of harmony. I, on the other hand, grew up in a household where arguments were loud and frequent. Our contrasting backgrounds led to significant challenges early in our marriage. While Paul tended to avoid conflict, my instinct was to confront issues head-on. It took time for us to understand each other's styles and find a balance that worked for both of us.

The Impact of Cultural Norms on Marital Dynamics

Cultural norms add another layer of complexity to conflict resolution. Different cultures have distinct expectations about roles, communication, and emotional expression in relationships. These expectations can clash in a marriage, especially when partners come from diverse backgrounds.

In Paul's culture, for instance, there was a strong emphasis on being polite, even at the expense of personal feelings. My culture, however, valued individual expression and direct communication.

This difference often led to misunderstandings. For example, when Paul would hold back his feelings to avoid confrontation, I interpreted it as indifference or a lack of care. Meanwhile, my direct approach sometimes felt overwhelming or disrespectful to him.

Navigating these differences required patience and a willingness to learn from each other. I had to recognize that Paul's preference for avoiding conflict was not meant to dismiss my feelings, while he learned that my confrontational style was rooted in a desire to address issues directly and resolve them.

Personal Anecdotes About Cultural Differences in Resolving Conflicts

Story 1: Hosting Gatherings

One memorable instance of our cultural differences arose during a disagreement about hosting gatherings. Paul believed hosting required meticulous preparation to create a welcoming environment, while I valued a more casual, spontaneous approach. His attention to detail — like

trimming bushes and preparing elaborate meals —
contrasted with my belief that our house was always
ready for guests, as my friends cared more about
spending time together than perfection.

When we hosted friends for the first time, Paul spent
days stressing over preparations, which I didn't
understand. I suggested we keep it simple, even
ordering takeout if necessary, but he felt
unappreciated for his efforts. This small difference in
expectations escalated into a heated argument. I
realized I couldn't change his approach entirely, so I
decided not to inform him too far in advance when
inviting friends over. This way, he wouldn't have too
much time to stress over details.

The compromise worked. While Paul didn't always
have time to prepare everything perfectly, he found
himself enjoying the gatherings too. By embracing
our differences, we both learned to approach these
moments with less stress and more appreciation for
their true purpose: strengthening our bond with
friends and each other.

Story 2: Sleeping Habit

Another early conflict that revealed our cultural and personal differences arose from how I slept. Paul and I had a small but significant disagreement about my sleeping habits. He slept on the left side of the bed while I slept on the right. My natural sleeping position was either on my back or on my right side, with my back facing Paul. One day, he told me that when I slept on my right side, it made him feel rejected.

I was taken aback. I explained that it wasn't intentional — I wasn't trying to reject him. That was simply how I felt most comfortable sleeping. But my explanation didn't satisfy him, and he got upset. I, in turn, grew frustrated. "Sleeping in the most comfortable position should be one of the most basic human rights," I told him angrily.

I couldn't understand why my choice of sleeping position, something so personal and instinctive, could upset him so much. Why did I even have to fight for such a basic right in my own marriage? His emotional reaction seemed unreasonable to me at the time.

Eventually, Paul gave in. He stopped being upset when I slept on my right side and accepted that it wasn't about him — it was just my habit. Looking back, I realized that his reaction wasn't really about the way I slept. It was about how he interpreted it emotionally. To him, my back being turned felt symbolic, as though I was closing myself off from him. While I didn't need to change my habit, his feelings weren't invalid — they just needed to be understood and talked through.

This small conflict taught us an important lesson: personal habits that seem insignificant to one person might carry emotional weight for the other. Open communication is essential for untangling these misunderstandings. It's not always about compromise — it's about understanding, accepting, and respecting each other's needs and boundaries.

Embracing Differences to Strengthen the Relationship

Acknowledging the role of cultural and personal backgrounds in conflict is not about assigning blame. It's about gaining insight into why we react the way we do and learning to respect each other's perspectives. By recognizing and embracing these differences, couples can turn potential sources of tension into opportunities for growth and connection.

In the next chapter, we will explore how recognizing and validating emotions can further strengthen a marriage by creating an environment of trust and empathy.

Chapter 3: The Danger of Avoidance

Avoiding conflict may feel like the easiest path to peace in a marriage, but it often leads to deeper, long-term problems. While the desire to sidestep disagreements is understandable — who wants to argue when you can keep the peace? — the cost of avoidance is far greater than it seems. Unspoken issues don't disappear; they fester beneath the surface, slowly eroding trust, intimacy, and connection. This chapter explores the hidden dangers of conflict avoidance and how it can ultimately create distance between partners.

The Sound System: A Lesson in Avoidance

It all started with something seemingly trivial: a sound system that flipped between TV and Alexa. Paul suggested a system where the person who finished using it would switch it to the other mode — TV to Alexa or vice versa — so it would be "ready" for the next person. At first glance, it sounded considerate, almost thoughtful. But I didn't agree.

To me, it made more sense for the person about to use the system to flip it themselves, avoiding unnecessary disruption. Paul's preference seemed kind on the surface, but in practice, it created a frustrating loop for both of us. If he finished watching TV and switched it to Alexa, but I didn't immediately need it, the system would sit in a mode I didn't want. Later, when I finally wanted to use the TV, I'd still have to flip it back. The same applied to him when I flipped it to TV after using Alexa.

This extra step wasn't helpful to either of us. It just added unnecessary effort. When I confronted Paul, I told him that his approach, while appearing considerate, was impractical and disrupted the natural flow of usage. Instead of being helpful, it created inefficiency. However, he didn't see it that way and stuck to his habit, believing it was a thoughtful gesture. What's worse, he began to bicker with me whenever I didn't follow his system or show appreciation for his so-called "kindness."

The tension grew. Every time I expressed my frustration, Paul would withdraw, trying to "let me win" because he believed I was losing control of my anger. To him, anger equaled irrationality, and his retreat was his way of de-escalating the situation. But to me, his actions felt dismissive. He wasn't listening to my concerns or engaging in the discussion. Instead, he was sidestepping the issue, leaving the underlying conflict unresolved.

Each time this happened, it felt like my emotions were being "managed" rather than understood. His temporary surrender wasn't genuine; it was a way to avoid engaging with the real problem. The more he "let me win," the more frustrated and alienated I felt.

Why Avoiding Conflict Feels Like the Right Choice

Conflict is uncomfortable. It stirs up emotions, challenges our sense of control, and sometimes leaves us feeling vulnerable. For many couples, avoiding disagreements seems like the best way to preserve harmony.

Paul believed avoiding conflict would keep our relationship harmonious, but in reality, it created a growing divide. His refusal to address the sound system issue wasn't just about flipping modes—it symbolized a broader habit of avoiding difficult conversations and dismissing my perspective.

- **Short-Term Relief, Long-Term Cost:** Avoiding conflict may offer immediate relief from tension, but unresolved issues resurface in unexpected ways, often creating bigger rifts over time.

- **The Illusion of Peace:** Silence or avoidance may seem like agreement, but it's not. True peace comes from resolution, not avoidance.

Avoidance often stems from a fear of confrontation — of being misunderstood, hurting our partner, or causing irreparable damage. Ironically, it is this fear that does the real harm, as unresolved issues compound over time.

The Cost of Avoiding Conflict

While avoiding conflict may seem harmless, it can have serious consequences for a marriage:

1. Emotional Distance

When conflicts are avoided, partners stop addressing what truly matters. Over time, they may begin to feel unheard or unimportant. This emotional gap can grow until partners feel more like roommates than a married couple.

2. Resentment

Unspoken grievances often turn into resentment. Without an outlet for expression, even small annoyances can build into significant barriers.

3. Loss of Trust

When one partner avoids conflict, the other may feel that their concerns are being dismissed. This undermines trust, as open communication is the foundation of a strong relationship.

4. Missed Opportunities for Growth

Conflict, when handled constructively, is an opportunity for growth and deeper understanding. Avoidance robs couples of these transformative moments.

The Turning Point

One day, after another argument about the sound system, I reached my breaking point. Frustrated and desperate, I told him, "I have never lost control of my anger. It would be an underestimation of me otherwise. I expressed it because I wanted you to face the issues that upset me. Ignoring our problems wouldn't help us grow. If you don't want to listen to me, our marriage won't last."

Something shifted in that moment. Paul realized that my anger wasn't out of control — it was a cry for him to face the issues that mattered to me. I wasn't angry about the sound system itself; it was about feeling unheard and undervalued. When he saw that I wasn't trying to "win" but rather pleading for us to work together, he finally stopped deflecting and "letting me win" just to end the fight.

That night, we had a real discussion. For the first time, he listened without interrupting and admitted he hadn't considered how his behavior affected me. He apologized and promised to address our disagreements more meaningfully in the future.

Others' Real-Life Examples: Couples Growing Apart Due to Avoidance

Example 1: Marianne and Steve

Marianne and Steve were the picture of harmony — or so it seemed. Whenever Marianne brought up concerns about their finances, Steve would wave her off, insisting everything was fine. Over time, Marianne stopped bringing up the topic altogether, feeling dismissed and unimportant. Years later, the financial strain exploded, but by then, the emotional distance between them had grown so vast that they no longer felt like partners. The issue wasn't just about money; it was about trust and communication. Their avoidance of conflict didn't preserve harmony; it quietly eroded trust and connection until it was too late.

Example 2: Joy and John

John believed the best way to keep Joy happy was to let her "win" every argument. He avoided disagreements, thinking he was protecting their relationship. But Joy began to notice that John rarely expressed his own opinions or needs. She felt like she was talking to a wall rather than a partner. She believed he didn't care and was not interested in their marriage. Without open communication, Joy felt isolated, and their marriage began to crumble. John's avoidance of conflict left Joy feeling isolated, proving that avoiding disagreements does more harm than facing them head-on.

Breaking the Cycle of Avoidance

1. Acknowledge the Pattern
Recognize avoidance as a problem. Understand that avoiding conflict may feel easier now but will lead to greater pain later.

2. Create a Safe Space
Establish a judgment-free environment where both partners feel comfortable expressing their concerns. Emphasize that addressing issues is about strengthening the relationship, not winning an argument.

3. Start Small
Begin by tackling smaller issues to build confidence in addressing conflicts. Success in resolving minor

disagreements can pave the way for discussing more challenging topics.

4. Focus on the Outcome

Remember that the goal of conflict resolution is not to "win" but to grow closer. Frame discussions as opportunities to improve your relationship.

Avoidance may feel like a way to keep the peace, but it only delays the inevitable. Unresolved issues grow into larger problems that threaten the foundation of a relationship. By choosing to face conflicts together, we learned to build a partnership rooted in trust, respect, and genuine connection.

From that day forward when Paul and I had thorough discussion about the sound system, Paul stopped flipping the sound system unnecessarily and abandoned his habit of bickering over minor issues. But more importantly, he began to see conflict not as something to avoid but as an opportunity to grow closer. That one conversation became a turning point in our marriage. It taught us that addressing conflicts head-on can lead to a deeper understanding and a stronger connection.

In the next chapter, we'll explore how recognizing and validating emotions plays a crucial role in navigating these difficult conversations.

Part 2: Recognizing and Validating Emotions

Chapter 4: Anger Is Not Out of Control

Anger is often misunderstood in relationships. Many people view it as a loss of control, a destructive force that should be avoided or suppressed. But anger, when expressed constructively, is not a loss of control. It's a natural emotional response that signals deeper issues needing attention. In this chapter, we'll explore how anger can be reframed as a valuable tool for growth and connection in marriage, rather than a threat.

Helping Your Spouse Understand That Expressing Anger Is Not a Loss of Control

One of the greatest misconceptions about anger is that it equals irrationality. For years, Paul believed that whenever I got angry, I had lost control. His instinctive response was to withdraw, thinking it was the best way to de-escalate the situation. But this only added to my frustration. His retreat felt dismissive, as though my feelings were unworthy of acknowledgment or discussion.

I had to repeatedly explain to Paul that my anger was never out of control. "It's not about losing control," I told him, "it's about expressing something important. When I get angry, I'm trying to address an issue that needs our attention." Slowly, he began to understand that anger wasn't the problem — the real issue was his avoidance of it.

When Paul finally stopped interpreting anger as a sign of irrationality, he was able to listen more openly. He began to realize that my frustration wasn't an attack on him but an invitation to address the root causes of our disagreements. This shift was pivotal in helping us build a stronger, more communicative relationship.

Reframing Anger as a Signal to Address Deeper Issues

Anger often carries valuable information about unmet needs or unresolved conflicts. Instead of viewing it as a destructive force, couples can learn to see it as a signal that something deeper is at play. For us, anger often revealed underlying issues that had gone unnoticed or unspoken.

For example, when Paul would dismiss my concerns or avoid addressing an issue, my anger would rise. It wasn't the surface disagreement that upset me but the underlying feeling of being unheard or invalidated. Recognizing this allowed us to move beyond the symptoms of our conflict and focus on the core issues. Anger became less about the frustration itself and more about the message it carried.

I once told Paul, "If I didn't care about us, I wouldn't get angry. My frustration comes from wanting us to grow and improve together. Ignoring these issues doesn't help us — it only makes me feel more distant from you." Framing my anger in this way helped him see it as an expression of care rather than hostility. It also encouraged him to engage with me more openly when I expressed frustration, rather than withdrawing.

Personal Stories of Making Paul Realize the True Purpose Behind Expressing Frustration

One memorable moment came during an argument about excessive spending. I had been frustrated for months because I felt he was spending on our backyard beyond our means. When I finally confronted Paul about it, he immediately withdrew, saying, "I don't want to fight about this."

This response only heightened my frustration. "I'm not fighting," I told him firmly, "I'm trying to communicate. When you ignore this conversation, it feels like you don't care about how I'm feeling." It took several conversations, but Paul eventually realized that my anger wasn't just about the excessive spending itself — it was about feeling unappreciated and unsupported. Once he understood this, we were able to have a productive discussion about how to spend money more carefully.

Another time, we had an argument about how we spent our weekends. I often wanted to relax at home, while Paul preferred going out and spending time at a shopping mall. My anger would flare when he insisted I should go with him, not because I didn't respect his preferences but because I felt we should respect each other's preferences. When I explained this to him, he began to see my frustration as a call for balance rather than a personal attack. We compromised by him going out on his own most of the time while I would go with him occasionally, which strengthened our bond and reduced tension in this area.

Embracing Anger as a Tool for Growth

When approached constructively, anger can be a powerful tool for growth in a relationship. It forces us to confront the issues that matter most and encourages deeper understanding and connection. For Paul and me, reframing anger as a signal rather than a threat transformed the way we communicated. We learned to listen, validate each other's emotions, and address underlying issues with compassion and respect.

The key to embracing anger is to focus on its purpose rather than its intensity. When couples view anger as a tool for addressing deeper issues, it becomes a catalyst for growth rather than a source of division. In the next chapter, we'll explore the importance of validation and how it can strengthen trust and intimacy in a marriage.

Chapter 5: The Danger of Underestimating Your Spouse

In a marriage, it can be all too easy to underestimate the emotional strength and resilience of your partner. This often happens when one partner dismisses the other's emotions or persistence in raising important issues. While it may seem harmless to downplay or ignore these moments, doing so can create lasting damage to trust, respect, and connection. In this chapter, we'll explore why underestimating your spouse's emotions is dangerous and how recognizing their strength can transform a marriage.

Why Dismissing a Partner's Emotions Is Harmful

Marriage is built on a foundation of mutual respect and understanding. When one partner dismisses the other's emotions, it undermines that foundation. The dismissed partner may feel invalidated, unheard, and even disrespected. Over time, this can lead to resentment and emotional distance, which weakens the bond between spouses.

Paul and I experienced this firsthand early in our marriage. Whenever I raised an issue that bothered me, Paul often brushed it off, saying things like, "It's not a big deal" or "You're overthinking it." To him, these statements were meant to reassure me and diffuse the situation. But to me, they felt dismissive. I wasn't asking him to solve the problem right away — I just wanted him to acknowledge my feelings and understand why the issue mattered to me.

One evening, after an argument about how we managed our finances, I told Paul, "When you dismiss my concerns, it's as if you're telling me I'm not worth listening to. I need to know that my feelings matter to you." That moment marked the beginning of a shift in our communication. Paul realized that by dismissing my emotions, he wasn't protecting our relationship from conflict — he was eroding my trust in him.

Learning to Accept Paul's Indirect "No"

Paul had a peculiar habit that frustrated me to no end: he would never say "no." Instead, he would respond with phrases like "not now," even when my request wasn't about "now" at all. At first, this drove me crazy. I prefer direct answers — a simple "yes" or "no" to a simple question. But with Paul, clarity was elusive.

Over time, I realized that this wasn't something he would change. His background as a salesman likely played a role. Salespeople are trained to avoid rejection and always keep the door open. I would joke, "I forgot, a salesperson can never say no." It became our inside joke, but the truth was, his indirectness often left me feeling unheard or uncertain.

Eventually, I learned to adapt. When I saw the pattern, I started saying it for him: "Ok, you won't." It helped me let go of the frustration and accept his roundabout way of answering. Even though I prefer direct communication, I've learned that his reluctance to say "no" isn't about avoiding me — it's about how he processes decisions. This acceptance has brought us more peace and understanding.

Recognizing and Respecting the Strength in a Spouse's Persistence

Persistence in raising issues is not a sign of weakness or nagging; it's often a demonstration of emotional strength and commitment to the relationship. When a spouse repeatedly brings up a concern, it's because they care deeply about resolving it and improving the connection between partners. Recognizing this persistence as a strength rather than an annoyance can transform the way couples approach conflict.

There was a time when I felt like I was constantly pushing Paul to discuss unresolved issues. Whether it was about dividing household responsibilities or making joint decisions about our future, I often felt like I was carrying the emotional weight of our relationship. At one point, Paul told me, "You're so stubborn about these things. Why can't you just let it go?" His words stung, but they also motivated me to explain why I persisted.

I said to him, "I bring these things up because I care about us. Ignoring them won't make them go away. It'll only make me feel more distant from you." Over time, Paul began to see my persistence as a sign of strength rather than criticism. He recognized that my willingness to address difficult topics was rooted in my commitment to our marriage, not a desire to nag or control him.

Embracing Mutual Respect and Understanding

Underestimating your spouse's emotions or persistence in addressing issues can create emotional barriers that are hard to overcome. By validating their feelings and acknowledging their strength, couples can foster a deeper sense of trust and connection.

Here are some practical steps to avoid underestimating your spouse:

1. Listen Actively

When your partner brings up an issue, listen with the intent to understand, not to respond. Avoid interrupting or dismissing their concerns.

2. Acknowledge Their Emotions

Even if you don't fully agree with your spouse's perspective, acknowledge the validity of their feelings. Statements like, "I can see why you feel that way" can go a long way in making them feel heard.

3. Express Gratitude for Their Persistence

Recognize that your spouse's persistence in addressing issues comes from a place of care and commitment. Thank them for bringing up difficult topics and working through them with you.

4. Reframe Challenges as Opportunities

Instead of viewing conflicts as obstacles, see them as opportunities to grow closer and strengthen your relationship.

By embracing these practices, couples can move past the dangers of underestimating each other and build a partnership rooted in mutual respect and understanding. Recognizing the emotional strength and persistence of your spouse is not just an act of kindness — it's a powerful way to deepen your connection and create a lasting, fulfilling marriage.

In the next chapter, we'll explore the value of validation and how it can strengthen trust and intimacy, even in the most challenging moments.

Chapter 6: The Value of Validation

Validation is one of the most powerful tools in a marriage. It goes beyond simply agreeing with your partner; it's about acknowledging and respecting their feelings, even when you don't fully understand or share their perspective. Validation creates a safe space for open communication, strengthens trust, and deepens intimacy. In this chapter, we'll explore strategies for validating your partner's emotions without feeling attacked and how this practice can transform your relationship.

Strategies to Validate Your Partner's Emotions Without Feeling Attacked

Validation doesn't mean you have to agree with everything your partner says or feels. It's about showing that you value their emotions and are willing to understand their perspective. Here are some practical strategies to help you validate your partner's emotions:

1. Listen Actively

Give your partner your full attention when they express their feelings. Avoid interrupting, and let them finish before responding. Active listening shows that you respect their need to be heard.

2. Acknowledge Their Emotions

Use phrases like, "I can see why you feel that way," or, "That sounds really frustrating," to demonstrate that you recognize their emotions as valid.

3. Avoid Defensiveness

When your partner shares something that feels critical, resist the urge to defend yourself immediately. Take a moment to understand their perspective before responding.

4. Reflect Back What You Hear

Paraphrase what your partner has said to ensure you understand their point of view. For example, "So you're saying that it upset you when I did X because it made you feel Y. Is that right?"

5. Separate Feelings from Solutions

Focus on validating your partner's emotions before jumping to problem-solving. Sometimes, they just want to feel heard, not "fixed."

How Validation Strengthens Trust and Intimacy

Validation is more than just a communication tool; it's a way of showing respect and care for your partner's inner world. When you validate your partner's emotions, you:

1. Build Trust

Your partner feels safe sharing their feelings without fear of judgment or dismissal.

2. Foster Intimacy

Emotional validation creates a deeper connection, as it shows that you genuinely care about your partner's experiences.

3. Reduce Conflict

Validation helps de-escalate disagreements by showing empathy and understanding, even in tense situations.

Story: Folding Socks

Paul takes care of the laundry in our house, and he folds his socks neatly in pairs before putting them in his drawer. I, on the other hand, simply place a pair of socks together without folding them when I store them in my drawer. Occasionally, Paul would fold my socks, too.

At first, I thanked him and gently told him not to fold my socks, as I preferred them unfolded. But sometimes, he would still fold my socks and say, "You're welcome," when I put them away without thanking him. I would respond, "I didn't thank you." To this, he'd reply, "Exactly the point." Annoyed, I'd retort, "You're a jerk."

Paul would get upset but refused to listen when I tried to explain my reasoning. Instead, he began accusing me of being ungrateful. The tension over something as small as socks grew unnecessarily. Eventually, I managed to make him listen: "If your intention was to get my appreciation, you already had it before I told you my preference. But after I told you I didn't want my socks folded, folding them doesn't help me.

It only shows that you're giving me what you want for me, not what I want. If you truly loved me and wanted to show kindness, you'd give me what I asked for instead of insisting on your way. If you keep doing what you want and expect my gratitude, it's not kindness — it's self-serving. That's why I called you a jerk."

Slowly, Paul began to understand. It took time, but he started to see that real kindness comes from respecting the other person's preferences — not just from doing something you think is kind.

Lessons from the Sock Story

This story highlights a crucial aspect of validation: true kindness and care come from understanding and respecting your partner's needs and preferences, not from imposing your own. Even small gestures, like folding socks, can carry emotional weight when they are tied to feelings of respect and appreciation.

Here's how validation played a role in resolving the conflict:

1. Recognizing Intentions:

I acknowledged that Paul's actions came from a place of wanting to help, even though they didn't align with my preferences.

2. Expressing My Needs Clearly

By explaining why I didn't want my socks folded, I helped Paul understand my perspective.

3. Learning Through Communication

Paul eventually recognized that respecting my preferences was more meaningful than continuing a gesture that felt dismissive to me.

Validation doesn't mean agreeing with everything your partner says or does. It means taking the time to understand their feelings and showing that their perspective matters. This practice can turn even small conflicts into opportunities for growth and connection.

In the next chapter, we'll explore how addressing conflicts head-on can turn disagreements into meaningful moments of understanding and strengthen your marriage.

Part 3: Facing Conflicts Head-On

Chapter 7: Why "Letting Your Spouse Win" Isn't Always Noble

In a marriage, conflicts are inevitable. How couples handle these conflicts can significantly impact the health of their relationship. One common approach is for one partner to "let the other win" to avoid further disagreement. While this might seem noble or selfless on the surface, it often creates more harm than good. "Letting your spouse win" can lead to unresolved issues, feelings of disconnection, and an imbalance in the relationship. This chapter explores the intentions behind this approach, why it can create distance, and how to distinguish between compromise and avoidance.

Examining the Intentions Behind "Letting the Other Win"

At first glance, "letting your spouse win" might seem like an act of love or sacrifice. Many people adopt this approach with good intentions, believing it's a way to maintain peace and show their partner they care. However, the underlying motivations often reveal a more complicated picture:

- **Avoiding Conflict**

  One partner may let the other win to avoid an argument, fearing that addressing the issue will lead to tension or emotional discomfort.

- **Preserving Harmony:**

  Some partners believe that by conceding, they are keeping the relationship harmonious. They might think, "If I let them have their way, we can avoid a fight."

- **Guilt or Insecurity:**

  A partner might feel guilty about standing their ground or insecure about expressing their true feelings, leading them to surrender.

While these intentions might seem selfless, they often mask deeper issues. Letting your spouse win isn't always a sign of generosity — it can be a way to sidestep important conversations or suppress one's own needs and desires.

Understanding Why This Approach Can Create Distance

The act of "letting your spouse win" might work temporarily, but over time, it can create emotional distance in the relationship. Here's why:

1. Unresolved Issues Persist

When one partner consistently concedes, the underlying problem doesn't go away. Instead, it festers, often resurfacing in more significant ways later.

2. Loss of Authenticity

If a partner is always conceding, they may begin to feel as though their voice doesn't matter. This can lead to feelings of resentment and a loss of authenticity in the relationship.

3. Erosion of Mutual Respect

A pattern of one partner always conceding can create an imbalance. The other partner might unknowingly begin to take their spouse's surrender for granted, weakening the mutual respect necessary for a healthy relationship. Or the other partner might think he/she doesn't care and is not interested in their marriage.

4. Emotional Disconnection

Over time, the partner who is always "letting the other win" may start to feel unseen or undervalued, leading to emotional disconnection and loneliness.

Differentiating Between Compromise and Avoidance

It's important to distinguish between healthy compromise and avoidance disguised as "letting your spouse win." While compromise involves mutual understanding and agreement, avoidance sidesteps the issue entirely. Here's how to tell the difference:

- **Compromise:** Both partners feel heard and respected. The solution reflects an effort to address both perspectives, even if neither gets exactly what they want. For example, if one partner wants to spend the weekend relaxing at home and the other wants to go out, a compromise might involve staying in one day and going out the next.

- **Avoidance:** One partner consistently surrenders to avoid conflict or discomfort. The other's perspective isn't acknowledged, and the underlying issue remains unresolved. For example, if one partner always concedes to the other's plans without discussion, they might feel invisible or ignored over time. Or the other partner may think he/she does not care and is not interested in their marriage.

Personal Story: Paul's Habit of Letting Me Win

Early in our marriage, Paul had a habit of letting me "win" whenever we argued. Whenever I got upset about something, he would withdraw, saying things like, "Fine, have it your way." At first, I thought this was his way of showing kindness or de-escalating the situation. But over time, it became clear that his withdrawal wasn't about generosity — it was about avoiding the issue entirely.

For example, if I expressed frustration about how household chores were divided, Paul would immediately agree to take on more responsibilities without really listening to my concerns. While his response seemed accommodating, it left me feeling unheard. I wasn't looking for him to simply agree; I wanted him to engage in a meaningful conversation about how we could share the workload in a way that felt fair to both of us.

I confronted Paul about his pattern of "letting me win." I told him, "When you give in without talking to me, it feels like you're not taking my feelings seriously. I'd rather have a real discussion and work through this together than feel like I'm forcing you into something." Paul gradually realized that his habit of letting me win wasn't helping our relationship — it was creating distance. We started having more open and honest discussions, which made us feel more connected and aligned as a couple.

Building a Relationship Based on Collaboration

To build a relationship where both partners feel valued and respected, it's essential to move away from avoidance and toward collaboration. Here are some strategies to foster healthy communication:

1. Engage in Meaningful Conversations

Instead of conceding, take the time to discuss the issue at hand. Ask questions, share your perspective, and seek to understand your partner's point of view.

2. Acknowledge Each Other's Needs

Recognize that both partners' needs and feelings are valid. A healthy relationship is built on mutual respect and understanding.

3. Be Honest About Your Intentions

If you find yourself letting your spouse win, reflect on why you're doing it. Are you avoiding conflict, or are you making a thoughtful compromise? Share your intentions with your partner to foster transparency.

4. Practice Healthy Compromise

Work together to find solutions that honor both perspectives. This might involve taking turns, trying new approaches, or finding creative ways to meet in the middle.

By replacing avoidance with collaboration, couples can create a stronger, more balanced relationship. Letting your spouse win might feel noble in the moment, but true partnership comes from addressing challenges together and working toward solutions that strengthen your bond.

In the next chapter, we'll explore strategies for addressing underlying issues in a marriage and how to set the stage for productive and respectful conversations.

Chapter 8: Strategies for Addressing Underlying Issues

Every conflict in a marriage has layers. While surface disagreements might seem straightforward, they often mask deeper, underlying issues. Addressing these root causes is essential for fostering understanding, trust, and long-term harmony in a relationship. In this chapter, we will explore how to identify the root causes of conflict, use effective communication techniques to discuss difficult topics, and set the stage for productive and respectful conversations.

How to Identify Root Causes of Conflict

The first step in addressing underlying issues is recognizing that the apparent problem is not always the real one. Beneath every argument lies deeper emotions, unmet needs, or unspoken expectations. Here are strategies to uncover the root causes of conflict:

1. Ask "Why" Questions

When a conflict arises, ask yourself and your partner, "Why does this matter to me?" or "Why am I feeling this way?" Digging deeper can help uncover the true source of tension.

2. Pay Attention to Patterns

Repeated arguments about similar topics often signal underlying issues. For instance, frequent disagreements about household chores might reveal unmet expectations about equality or appreciation.

3. Reflect on Emotional Triggers

Notice what emotions arise during conflicts. Anger, frustration, or sadness can indicate deeper feelings of being unheard, unvalued, or misunderstood.

4. Consider Individual Histories

Personal experiences and upbringing can shape how each partner perceives and reacts to conflict. Reflecting on these influences can help explain recurring issues.

Communication Techniques to Discuss Difficult Topics

Once you've identified the root causes of conflict, the next step is addressing them constructively. Effective communication is key to resolving deeper issues. Here are techniques to help:

1. Use "I" Statements

Frame your concerns in terms of your own feelings and needs rather than blaming your partner. For example, instead of saying, "You never listen to me," try, "I feel unheard when I share my thoughts, and it's important to me that we have open communication."

2. Practice Active Listening

Give your partner your full attention when they speak. Avoid interrupting or formulating your response while they're talking. Instead, focus on understanding their perspective.

3. Paraphrase and Reflect

After your partner shares their feelings, repeat back what you heard to confirm your understanding. For example, "It sounds like you feel overwhelmed when I ask for help with the kids because you're already juggling a lot. Is that right?"

4. Stay Calm and Manage Emotions

Heated discussions can escalate quickly. If emotions run high, take a break and agree to revisit the conversation once both of you are calm.

5. Focus on Solutions, Not Blame

Instead of dwelling on past mistakes, shift the conversation toward finding solutions that work for both partners. Ask, "How can we address this together?"

Setting the Stage for Productive and Respectful Conversations

Creating the right environment for difficult discussions can make all the difference. Here are strategies to ensure your conversations are respectful and productive:

1. Choose the Right Time and Place

Avoid discussing sensitive topics when one or both partners are stressed, tired, or distracted. Find a quiet, private space where you can talk without interruptions.

2. Establish Ground Rules

Agree on basic rules for communication, such as no interrupting, no name-calling, and no bringing up unrelated past issues.

3. Show Empathy and Respect

Approach the conversation with a genuine desire to understand your partner's feelings and perspective. Even if you disagree, acknowledge their emotions as valid.

4. Use Positive Reinforcement

Highlight the progress you've made together and express appreciation for your partner's willingness to engage in the discussion. For example, "I really appreciate that you're taking the time to talk about this with me."

5. Take Responsibility for Your Role

Acknowledge your own contributions to the conflict. This demonstrates accountability and encourages your partner to do the same.

Example: Revisiting the Sound System Conflict

A good example of this happened with the sound system conflict I shared earlier. What initially appeared to be about flipping modes turned out to reflect deeper feelings about thoughtfulness and respect. Once we identified the root cause, we were able to address the issue productively.

This approach can work for many seemingly minor disagreements. When couples dig deeper, they often uncover hidden emotions or unmet needs that drive their frustrations. By focusing on the root cause rather than the surface issue, conflicts become opportunities for deeper understanding.

Turning Conflicts into Opportunities for Growth

Addressing underlying issues requires patience, empathy, and a willingness to engage in meaningful conversations. By identifying root causes, using effective communication techniques, and setting the stage for respectful discussions, couples can transform conflicts into opportunities for growth and connection.

In the next chapter, we'll explore the power of persistence in resolving conflicts and how standing firm can lead to deeper understanding and a stronger marriage.

Chapter 9: The Power of Persistence

Persistence is often misunderstood in relationships. It's sometimes dismissed as nagging or stubbornness, but in reality, persistence can be a powerful force for positive change. When approached with respect and care, standing firm on important issues can strengthen a marriage and lead to deeper understanding. In this chapter, we'll explore stories of couples who benefited from addressing conflicts head-on and discuss why staying persistent, yet respectful, is essential for resolving issues and fostering connection.

Stories of Couples Who Benefited from Facing Conflicts Together

Jane and Michael: Balancing Career and Family

Jane and Michael had a recurring conflict about how to balance their demanding careers with family time. Jane felt that Michael prioritized his job over their relationship and their children, often working late and missing important family events. Michael, on the other hand, believed he was providing for the family and couldn't understand why Jane didn't appreciate his efforts.

Instead of giving up on the issue, Jane persisted in addressing her concerns. She stood firm but approached the topic with empathy. Rather than blaming Michael, she shared how his absence made her and the children feel. "I know you're working hard for us, and I appreciate that," she said. "But the kids need you, and I need you. Can we find a way to balance this better?"

Over time, Michael began to see the impact his work habits were having on his family. He adjusted his schedule to spend more time at home and even started turning down projects that required excessive travel. Their persistence in having this difficult conversation paid off, leading to a healthier balance and a stronger relationship.

Sarah and Alex: Sharing Household Responsibilities

For years, Sarah felt like she was carrying the burden of managing their home while Alex didn't contribute as much. Whenever she brought it up, Alex would agree to help but never followed through, leading to frustration on both sides.

Instead of letting the resentment fester, Sarah decided to tackle the issue head-on. She approached Alex with specific examples of tasks she needed help with and explained how the imbalance made her feel overwhelmed. She persisted in revisiting the conversation whenever Alex fell back into old habits, but she did so calmly and respectfully.

Alex eventually realized that his lack of follow-through wasn't just about chores — it was about showing respect and appreciation for Sarah's efforts. He began taking more initiative around the house, and Sarah's persistence transformed a source of tension into an opportunity for growth and partnership.

The Importance of Standing Firm While Staying Respectful

Standing firm in a relationship doesn't mean being confrontational or refusing to compromise. It's about expressing your needs and values clearly, even when it's uncomfortable, and doing so in a way that respects your partner's perspective. Here's why persistence is so important:

1. Shows Commitment to the Relationship

Persisting on an issue demonstrates that you care enough about the relationship to address what matters. It's a way of saying, "I value us enough to work through this."

2. Encourages Growth and Change

Avoiding conflict can lead to stagnation, while persistence creates opportunities for growth. When couples address issues together, they learn more about each other and strengthen their bond.

3. Builds Mutual Respect

Standing firm, when done respectfully, shows your partner that your feelings and needs are important. It also sets the tone for open, honest communication.

4. Prevents Resentment

Addressing conflicts head-on helps prevent the buildup of resentment, which can erode trust and intimacy over time.

Strategies for Being Persistent Without Being Overbearing

1. Choose the Right Timing

Bring up difficult topics when both partners are calm and receptive. Avoid discussing sensitive issues during moments of stress or exhaustion.

2. Focus on the Issue, Not the Person

Keep the conversation centered on the problem at hand rather than attacking your partner's character. For example, say, "I feel overwhelmed when I'm managing everything alone," rather than, "You never help me."

3. Be Specific

Vague complaints can feel like criticism. Instead, offer specific examples and actionable solutions. For instance, "Can we set aside time on Sunday to plan the week together?" is more constructive than "You're always disorganized."

4. Acknowledge Progress

When your partner makes an effort, acknowledge it. Positive reinforcement encourages continued growth and cooperation.

5. Know When to Pause

Persistence doesn't mean pushing relentlessly. If a conversation becomes heated, take a break and revisit the issue later. This shows respect for both your partner's emotions and the relationship.

Personal Story: Persistence in Addressing Financial Issues

Paul and I had ongoing disagreements about how to manage our finances. He often piled up credit card debts without consulting me.

At first, I let it slide, thinking it wasn't worth the argument. But over time, these debts added up, and the lack of communication began to bother me deeply. I decided to address the issue directly. I told Paul, "When you pile up credit debts, you are damaging our finances."

Paul dismissed my concerns as overreacting at first. But I didn't give up. I continued to bring it up, calmly and consistently, explaining how important collaboration was to me. Eventually, Paul began to see the pattern and understood why it mattered. We agreed to discuss a solution together moving forward, which brought us closer and strengthened our partnership.

Turning Persistence Into Growth

Persistence is not about winning an argument or getting your way. It's about standing firm on the things that matter most while maintaining respect and empathy for your partner. When couples approach conflict with persistence and care, they turn disagreements into opportunities for deeper connection and mutual growth.

In the next chapter, we'll explore how turning heated discussions into growth opportunities can transform even the most challenging conflicts into moments of profound understanding and intimacy.

Part 4: Building a Stronger Relationship

Chapter 10: Turning Heated Discussions into Growth Opportunities

Conflict in marriage is often viewed as something to be avoided, but when handled constructively, disagreements can lead to deeper understanding, stronger connection, and personal growth. Rather than seeing heated discussions as destructive, couples can learn to use these moments as opportunities to strengthen their communication and relationship. In this chapter, we'll explore how conflicts can deepen mutual understanding, provide practical tips for resolving disputes constructively, and highlight the importance of celebrating small victories in communication.

How Conflicts Can Deepen Mutual Understanding

While conflicts can be uncomfortable, they often reveal important insights about each partner's feelings, needs, and values. When couples engage with each other honestly and openly during disagreements, they create an opportunity to learn and grow together.

1. Conflicts Reveal What Truly Matters

Heated discussions often highlight underlying issues or unmet needs. For example, an argument about household chores may reveal a deeper need for appreciation or fairness.

2. Conflicts Encourage Vulnerability

When partners share their frustrations, they often expose feelings they've been holding back. This vulnerability, though difficult, creates an opportunity to build trust and intimacy.

3. Conflicts Foster Growth Through Resolution

Working through disagreements forces couples to listen, empathize, and find solutions that respect both perspectives. Successfully navigating these moments deepens mutual respect and understanding.

Rather than avoiding conflict, couples who face issues head-on are better able to understand each other's values, strengthen their bond, and prevent resentment from festering.

Practical Tips for Resolving Disputes Constructively

Handling heated discussions constructively requires effort, patience, and a willingness to prioritize the relationship over "winning" the argument. Here are practical tips to turn conflicts into opportunities for growth:

1. Stay Calm and Take Breaks When Needed

If emotions run too high, it's okay to pause the conversation. Step back, take a few deep breaths, and return to the discussion when you're both calmer. Say, "I'm feeling too upset to talk right now. Let's take a break and revisit this when we're ready."

2. Listen to Understand, Not to Respond

Focus on truly understanding your partner's perspective instead of formulating your next response. Listening shows respect and creates space for empathy.

3. Use "I" Statements

Frame your concerns in a way that expresses your feelings without blaming. For example, "I feel overwhelmed when I manage everything alone" is more constructive than "You never help me."

4. Avoid Escalating the Conflict

Stay away from name-calling, yelling, or bringing up unrelated past issues. Focus on the topic at hand and treat each other with kindness and respect.

5. Find Common Ground

Identify areas where you both agree and build solutions from there. Compromise is not about one person winning and the other losing; it's about finding a solution that works for both of you.

6. Look for the Lesson in the Conflict

After resolving a disagreement, reflect on what you learned about yourself, your partner, and your relationship. Use the experience as a stepping stone for growth.

Personal Story: Turning Arguments Into Growth

One evening, Paul and I had a heated discussion about how we spent our weekends. Paul wanted to go out and socialize, while I preferred staying home to relax. At first, our conversation escalated into frustration. I accused him of not respecting my need for downtime, and he insisted I was being antisocial. Both of us felt unheard, and the conversation quickly spiraled into a tense argument.

At that moment, I decided to pause and change my approach. I said, "Let's take a moment. I want to understand why this matters to you." When we revisited the conversation calmly, I listened as Paul shared how going out energized him and made him feel connected to others. In turn, I explained that my preference to stay home wasn't about avoiding him but about feeling relaxed and lazy.

This exchange turned what began as a heated discussion into an opportunity for growth. Paul and I found a compromise: we would spend some weekends socializing and others relaxing at home.

By listening to each other's needs and being willing to find common ground, we turned a recurring conflict into a chance to better understand and support one another.

Celebrating Small Victories in Communication

Progress in communication doesn't always come in the form of major breakthroughs. Often, it's the small victories that matter most—moments when both partners listen, empathize, and work toward a solution together.

1. Recognize Efforts, Not Just Outcomes

Celebrate the effort your partner puts into communicating and resolving issues, even if the outcome isn't perfect. Acknowledging progress encourages continued growth.

2. Appreciate Moments of Calm and Respect

If you manage to have a difficult conversation without escalating into anger or blame, that's a victory worth celebrating.

3. Learn from Each Conversation

Reflect on what worked well in your discussion and apply those lessons to future conflicts. For example, if taking a break helped you de-escalate a tense moment, use that strategy again next time.

4. Share Gratitude

Express gratitude for your partner's willingness to engage in difficult conversations. A simple, "Thank you for talking this through with me" can go a long way in strengthening trust and intimacy.

Transforming Conflict Into Connection

Heated discussions don't have to weaken a marriage. When approached with patience, respect, and a focus on understanding, conflicts can deepen the connection between partners. By learning to resolve disputes constructively and celebrating small victories along the way, couples can transform even the most challenging conversations into opportunities for growth.

In the next chapter, we'll explore how rebuilding trust and intimacy after conflicts can help couples emerge stronger and more connected than before.

Chapter 11: Rebuilding Trust and Intimacy

Every marriage faces moments of strain. Disagreements, misunderstandings, or breaches of trust can shake the foundation of a relationship, leaving both partners feeling disconnected. However, these challenges can also be opportunities to rebuild trust and deepen intimacy. In this chapter, we will explore the role of forgiveness and empathy in resolving conflicts, practical exercises for rebuilding trust after disagreements, and how to recognize and celebrate growth and resilience as a couple.

The Role of Forgiveness and Empathy in Resolving Conflicts

Forgiveness and empathy are essential components of healing and rebuilding trust in a marriage. Without them, resentment and emotional distance can take root, eroding the connection between partners.

1. Forgiveness as a Choice

- Forgiveness doesn't mean forgetting or condoning hurtful actions. It's a conscious decision to let go of resentment and move forward together. Forgiveness allows both partners to focus on rebuilding rather than dwelling on the past.

- Christians are called to forgive as God's grace through us. We choose to forgive even if our spouses do not deserve it, just as we don't deserve Jesus's salvation. In my marriage, choosing to forgive has not always been easy, but it has allowed me to show grace when Paul — or I — needed it most. It's a reminder that our love, like God's grace, can overcome even the hardest moments when we trust and lean into it.

2. Empathy as a Bridge

- Empathy helps partners see the situation from each other's perspective. By understanding the feelings and motivations behind your spouse's actions, it becomes easier to approach the conflict with compassion and openness.

3. The Connection Between Forgiveness and Empathy

- Empathy fosters forgiveness by humanizing your partner and reducing the tendency to assign blame. When both partners practice empathy, they create a foundation of mutual understanding and support.

Exercises to Rebuild Trust After Disagreements

Rebuilding trust takes time and intentional effort. These exercises can help couples repair their bond and strengthen their connection:

1. Open and Honest Communication

- Set aside time to talk openly about the conflict and its impact on your relationship. Use active listening and "I" statements to share your feelings without placing blame. For example, "I felt hurt when you didn't consult me about that decision because it made me feel excluded."

2. Daily Check-Ins

- Create a routine of short daily conversations to share thoughts, feelings, and experiences. This practice helps maintain open communication and rebuilds emotional closeness over time.

3. Apology and Accountability

- A sincere apology can go a long way in rebuilding trust. Acknowledge your role in the conflict and express a genuine desire to make amends. For example, "I'm sorry for dismissing your concerns. I realize now how important they are to you, and I'll do better moving forward."

4. Trust-Building Activities

- Engage in activities that require collaboration and mutual reliance, such as cooking a meal together, planning a trip, or tackling a home project. These shared experiences reinforce teamwork and trust.

5. Reassurance Through Actions

- Rebuilding trust often requires consistent, trustworthy behavior. Follow through on promises, demonstrate reliability, and show your partner that they can depend on you.

Recognizing Growth and Resilience as a Couple

As couples work through challenges, it's important to acknowledge the progress they've made and the strength they've developed together. Recognizing growth and resilience fosters gratitude and reinforces the bond between partners.

1. Celebrate Milestones
- Reflect on moments where you overcame conflicts or grew stronger as a couple. Celebrating these milestones reminds both partners of their shared journey and accomplishments.

2. Focus on Strengths
- Highlight the qualities that make your relationship resilient, such as patience, perseverance, or effective communication. Recognizing these strengths builds confidence in your ability to navigate future challenges.

3. Practice Gratitude

*   Express gratitude for your partner's efforts and commitment to the relationship. Simple gestures, like saying "Thank you for being patient with me" or "I'm grateful for how you supported me during that tough time," reinforce positivity and appreciation.

4. Reflect on Lessons Learned

*   Use past conflicts as learning opportunities. Ask yourselves, "What did we learn from this experience?" and "How did it make us stronger as a couple?" Recognizing growth helps reframe challenges as opportunities for connection.

Personal Story: Rebuilding After a Financial Disagreement

One of the most challenging moments in our marriage came after a heated disagreement about finances. Paul piled up huge credit card debts again.

After the argument, we took time to reflect separately. I knew that avoiding this conversation would only make things worse, so I chose to confront it directly, no matter how difficult it was. When we finally sat down to talk, I insisted we would take out a second mortgage to pay off all the credit card debts — with one condition. Paul would not accumulate a single penny of credit card debt again. I said firmly, "If you can't pay the full statement amount on the due date, then you can't make a purchase. This will be our agreement, and our marriage will depend on it solely."

Paul listened quietly, clearly taken aback, but he didn't interrupt. He knew I don't make empty threats — and this was no exception. After a moment, he admitted his mistake and said, "I understand. I'm sorry for what I've done, and I won't let this happen again."" His willingness to take accountability and sincerely apologize was a turning point for us both.

This experience reminded us that trust isn't rebuilt overnight — it requires clear boundaries, accountability, and consistent effort. Paul knew my insistence came from a place of love and honesty; I don't make empty threats, and he understood the importance of my stance. When both partners commit to the process, the relationship can emerge stronger than ever.

This experience taught us the importance of collaboration and reinforced our commitment to each other. While it took time to fully rebuild trust, the process brought us closer and strengthened our partnership.

Moving Forward Together

Rebuilding trust and intimacy after a conflict isn't easy, but it's possible with forgiveness, empathy, and intentional effort. By engaging in trust-building exercises, acknowledging growth, and practicing gratitude, couples can repair their bond and emerge stronger than before.

In the next chapter, we'll explore how conflict itself can become a foundation for a successful marriage and a deeper connection between partners.

Chapter 12: Conflict as a Foundation for a Successful Marriage

At first glance, conflict may seem like the enemy of a happy marriage. It's uncomfortable, emotionally draining, and often avoided at all costs. However, couples who learn to face conflicts together and work through them constructively often discover that these moments of struggle become the very foundation of a stronger, more resilient marriage. In this chapter, we will explore how conflicts can lead to growth, why embracing conflict is an opportunity rather than a threat, and share personal reflections on the transformation of our own marriage.

Why Couples Who Work Through Conflicts Grow Stronger

Conflict reveals what truly matters to each partner. It uncovers deeper values, unmet needs, and hidden vulnerabilities. By working through disagreements rather than avoiding them, couples build trust, strengthen communication, and deepen their understanding of one another.

1. Conflict Builds Trust

Trust is not built in moments of harmony; it is forged in times of difficulty. When couples face a conflict and come out the other side together, they reinforce their belief in each other's commitment and willingness to grow.

2. Conflict Improves Communication

Effective conflict resolution requires listening, understanding, and expressing oneself clearly. Each time couples navigate disagreements successfully, they improve their communication skills, making future conflicts easier to handle.

3. Conflict Fosters Emotional Intimacy

Vulnerability during conflict allows partners to see each other's true emotions. Sharing frustrations, fears, and hopes — and feeling heard — creates a deeper emotional bond.

4. Conflict Encourages Growth

Conflict challenges couples to step outside their comfort zones, reflect on their behavior, and seek solutions together. These experiences foster personal growth and strengthen the partnership.

Rather than viewing conflict as a threat to harmony, couples can choose to see it as a necessary part of building a strong and healthy relationship.

Embracing Conflict as an Opportunity Rather Than a Threat

When handled poorly, conflicts can drive a wedge between partners. But when approached constructively, they become opportunities for growth and connection. Here are ways to reframe conflict as a positive force:

1. Shift Your Perspective

View conflict as a chance to understand your partner better. Instead of asking, "Why are we fighting?" ask, "What can I learn from this disagreement?"

2. Focus on Solutions, Not Blame

Avoid getting stuck in cycles of blame or defensiveness. Focus instead on finding solutions that address both partners' needs.

3. See Conflict as a Form of Investment

Just like exercising a muscle, working through conflict builds a stronger relationship. It may be uncomfortable, but the long-term benefits far outweigh the temporary discomfort.

4. Celebrate Progress

After resolving a disagreement, take time to reflect on what you learned and how it brought you closer. Recognizing growth reinforces the value of facing conflicts together.

Personal Reflections on the Transformation of Our Own Marriage

In our marriage, conflicts were once a source of frustration and emotional distance. Paul's instinct to avoid arguments and my persistence in confronting issues often created a cycle of misunderstanding. For a long time, I saw conflict as a problem to be fixed, while Paul saw it as something to be avoided entirely. It wasn't until we began to reframe conflict as an opportunity that we started to see real change.

I remember one of the turning points in our marriage — the conflict over the sound system. At first, it felt like a trivial issue, but it revealed something deeper: Paul's desire to show kindness in his way and my frustration with feeling unheard. It took many heated discussions, but eventually, we both learned valuable lessons. Paul realized that avoiding conflict didn't make the problem disappear, and I learned to express my frustration in ways that helped him understand rather than withdraw. That small conflict taught us how to navigate disagreements constructively and brought us closer as a couple.

Another moment of transformation came during our disagreement over finances. When I confronted Paul about his credit card debt, I set clear boundaries and told him the future of our marriage depended on us resolving the issue. I didn't make empty threats — Paul knew I meant every word. This conflict forced both of us to face uncomfortable truths. Paul took accountability, and we worked together to create a plan for our financial future. What started as a painful disagreement became a catalyst for growth, trust, and teamwork.

Through these and other experiences, I learned that conflict itself wasn't the enemy — it was our fear of addressing it. Once we embraced conflict as an opportunity to communicate, grow, and reconnect, our marriage began to transform. Heated discussions no longer signaled doom; they became a pathway to deeper understanding and intimacy.

Moving Forward: Building a Marriage That Thrives on Growth

Conflict, when approached with love, patience, and respect, can become the foundation for a successful marriage. It is not something to fear or avoid but rather an opportunity to learn, adapt, and grow together. Couples who work through their conflicts build a relationship grounded in trust, communication, and resilience.

Here are final reminders for embracing conflict as a foundation for your marriage:

1. Face Conflicts Head-On

Avoiding conflict may feel easier in the moment, but it leads to long-term frustration and distance. Choose to face issues with honesty and care.

2. Learn from Each Conflict

Reflect on the lessons each disagreement teaches you. What did you learn about yourself, your partner, and your relationship?

3. Reframe Conflict as an Opportunity

See each disagreement as a chance to strengthen your marriage, improve communication, and deepen your connection.

4. Celebrate the Growth

After working through a difficult issue, celebrate your progress as a couple. Acknowledge the effort, patience, and love that brought you closer.

Final Thoughts

Conflict is not a threat to a successful marriage — it's a necessary ingredient. When approached with mutual respect and a willingness to grow, conflicts can transform a relationship, bringing partners closer than ever before. Our marriage is stronger today not because we avoided conflict, but because we learned to embrace it as a tool for growth, trust, and deeper love.

May you face your own conflicts with courage, knowing that every disagreement is an opportunity to build a stronger, more fulfilling partnership.

Conclusion

Conflict is an inevitable part of every marriage, but it doesn't have to be something to fear or avoid. When approached with a spirit of love, patience, and understanding, conflict can become a powerful tool for growth, connection, and transformation. The key is to embrace disagreements as opportunities rather than threats, using them to build trust, deepen communication, and strengthen the bond between partners.

A Call to Action

If there is one message to take away from this book, it is this: don't shy away from the hard conversations. Avoiding conflict may seem like a way to maintain peace, but it often creates distance and unresolved tension. By choosing to address conflicts head-on, you demonstrate your commitment to the relationship and your willingness to grow together.

Remember, anger and frustration are not the enemies. They are signals pointing to deeper issues that need attention. Rather than suppressing these emotions, use them to spark honest, respectful dialogue. Approach every disagreement with the goal of understanding, not winning. By doing so, you create an environment where both partners feel valued, heard, and respected.

Final Thoughts

Marriage is not about the absence of conflict but about how couples handle it. Every disagreement offers an opportunity to learn more about each other, to adapt, and to grow closer. When both partners commit to navigating conflicts constructively, they lay the foundation for a relationship built on trust, resilience, and mutual respect.

In our own journey, we discovered that facing conflict together transformed our marriage. Heated discussions that once created frustration became stepping stones to deeper understanding and intimacy. Through every challenge, we learned to communicate better, respect each other's perspectives, and celebrate our progress as a couple.

To all the couples reading this: embrace the hard moments. Let them shape you and your relationship into something stronger and more beautiful. Know that every conflict, when met with courage and compassion, is an opportunity to create a marriage where both partners feel truly connected and deeply loved.

May your journey together be filled with growth, understanding, and the enduring joy of a relationship that thrives not despite conflict, but because of it.

About the Author

Hope Grace is an author, translator, and editor with a passion for empowering others through her writing. With a background as a Senior IT Security Analyst, Hope combines her analytical approach with a deep understanding of human relationships to deliver insights that resonate with readers.

Originally from China, Hope's personal journey as an immigrant and her experiences navigating cultural and personal differences have shaped her perspectives on communication, conflict resolution, and resilience in relationships. Her ability to address challenging topics with honesty and clarity shines through in her writing.

In addition to her professional work, Hope is the author of several books, including *Horizon Shift: Inspired by Zhang's Unified Field Theory*, *Voyage Throught Planet Guoke: Inspired by the True Experiences of Zhang XiangQian*, *From Passive to Passion: A Chinese Immigrant's Journey to American Activism*, *One-Way Relationships: The*

Path to Joy, Resilience, and Wholeness, and *Save $1M in Retirement: My Journey That Everyone Can Follow.* Her works explore themes of personal growth, empowerment, and the pursuit of understanding in all aspects of life.

Hope's insights are rooted not only in her personal experiences but also in her commitment to sharing practical wisdom that inspires change. She believes that conflict, when approached with love and persistence, can transform relationships and strengthen the bonds that matter most.

When she's not writing, Hope enjoys connecting with her readers, exploring new ideas, and staying active on her fitness YouTube channel, *Age Gracefully with Hope.* She resides in Alexandria, Virginia, with her family.

Learn more about her work at HopeGracePublishing.com.

.

www.ingramcontent.com/pod-product-compliance
Lightning Source LLC
Chambersburg PA
CBHW020319130626
46549CB00003B/934